1,001
WAYS
TO
MOTIVATE
YOURSELF
AND OTHERS

TO GET WHERE YOU WANT TO GO

D0711738

1,001
WAYS
TO
MOTIVATE

YOURSELF
AND OTHERS

TO GET WHERE YOU WANT TO GO

Sang H. Kim Ph.D.

Turtle Press
Hartford

1,001 WAYS TO MOTIVATE YOURSELF AND OTHERS

Turtle Press

Turtle Press paperback edition / September 1996
12 printings through March 1999

Turtle Press books may be purchased for educational, self-help, business, or
promotional use. For information or to contact the author please write:
>   Turtle Press
>   P.O. Box 290206
>   Wethersfield CT 06129-0206
>   1-800-778-8785
>   1-860-721-1198 (outside of U.S.A.)

Library of Congress Card Catalog Number 95-31912
ISBN   1-880336-07-3
First Edition

Library of Congress Cataloguing in Publication Data

Kim, Sang H.
>   1,001 ways to motivate yourself and others / by Sang H. Kim.
>>   p.   cm.
>   ISBN 1-880336-07-3 (pbk.)
>   1. Motivation (psychology)   2. Success -- Psychological aspects.
>   I Title.
>   BF503.K525   1995
>   153.8 - - dc20   95-31912

PRINTED IN THE UNITED STATES OF AMERICA

Contents

Chapter One: The Roots of Motivation **9**
    Survival vs. Achievement 10
    What Motivates? 11
    Needs and Priorities 12
    Actions Rewarded 12
    Conditioned Response 14
    Motivation or Manipulation? 15
    Theories of Motivation 17
    Using this Book 20

Chapter Two: 160 Ways to Motivate Yourself **25**
    Inspiration 26
    Application 31

Chapter Three: 60 Ways to Motivate Your Boss **43**
    Inspiration 44
    Application 45

Chapter Four: 111 Ways to Motivate your Employees **53**
    Inspiration 54
    Application 56

Chapter Five: 75 Ways to Motivate your Team **67**
    Inspiration 68
    Application 69

Chapter Six: 54 Ways to Motivate your Students **77**
    Inspiration 78
    Application 79

Chapter Seven: 56 Ways to Motivate your Peers **87**
    Inspiration 88
    Application 89

Chapter Eight: 50 Ways to Motivate your Clients & Customers 97
    Inspiration 98
    Application 99

Chapter Nine: 75 Ways to Motivate Change 107
    Motivate Yourself 108
    Motivate Others 113

Chapter Ten: 30 Ways to Motivate Conflict Resolution .. 119
    Inspiration 120
    Application 120

Chapter Eleven: 56 Ways to Motivate Creativity 125
    Inspiration 126
    Application 128

Chapter Twelve: 44 Ways to Motivate Decision Making 133
    Inspiration 134
    Application 136

Chapter Thirteen: 95 Ways to Motivate Success 141
    Inspiration 142
    Application 145

Chapter Fourteen: 39 Ways to Motivate Leadership 153
    Inspiration 154
    Application 155

Chapter Fifteen: 95 Ways to Motivate Productivity 161
    Inspiration 162
    Application 163

Chapter One

The Roots of Motivation

The
Roots
of Motivation

Motivation is a force that creates behavior to fulfill a need. It is not necessarily positive or negative, fulfilling or frustrating. It can be all, some or none of these. When motivation is mentioned, an image springs to mind of a coach giving his team a fiery pep talk, of a sales manager rallying his sales force, of a marathon runner setting out to train on the coldest day of the year. However, motivation is not just about heroic feats of positive action.

How often have you heard the phrase "Police are still searching for a motive."? Yes, people can also be motivated to take negative actions. Someone can be motivated to commit a crime, overthrow authority, sabotage a rival or seek revenge. This is the darker side of human motivation, but it is motivation just the same.

Motivation is a powerful and complex force that causes us to act. Motivation itself is not an observable phenomenon, but the force behind the resulting behavior. One behavior can have many possible motives. For instance, a man can be motivated to exercise because he wants to look more muscular, because he is suffering from heart disease, because he is under a lot of stress, because he wants to socialize more, because he is training for an athletic event, because he likes to feel healthy, because he wants to lose weight, because he wants to meet women interested in fitness, or simply because he likes exercising.

What we see is not his motivation, but the external results of that motivation manifested in his desire to exercise. Understanding the underlying motive behind the action is the key to motivating anyone, including yourself. Imagine you are a personal fitness trainer and a young woman comes to you for guidance in setting up an exercise plan. Without knowing what her motives are for exercising, you cannot effectively design a plan to keep her motivated to exercise. If she is training for a marathon and you give her an intense weight lifting plan, she will view the regiment you have designed for her as irrelevant to reaching her goal. Knowing what she wants to achieve is essential in motivating her to achieve her goals.

Survival vs. Achievement

Basically there are two levels of motivation: survival and achievement. Survival needs include safety, nourishment, shelter, and procreation. These fundamental physical needs must be fulfilled to satisfy our bodies' daily requirements. Once these basic needs are satisfied, we begin to look to other areas of need including achievement, emotional fulfillment, personal growth, and self-worth. It is these higher emotional and spiritual needs that we address when we speak of motivating others.

The key to motivating a person into action lies in knowing which of these needs is most prominent in that person at a particular point in time. Motivating forces are not universal. They are subjective and can change at a moments notice as priorities change. What motivates today may seem hollow and useless tomorrow.

What Motivates?

Below is a list of the emotions and needs that ignite people to action:

Achievement
Acquisition
Advancement
Affiliation
Ambition
Anger
Attention
Autonomy
Balance
Belonging
Betrayal
Camaraderie
Challenge
Change
Closure
Compassion
Confidence
Consistency
Construction
Control
Cooperation
Creation
Deception
Decisiveness
Defense
Desperation
Education

Ego
Enjoyment
Esteem
Excitement
Fairness
Fear
Forgiveness
Freedom
Giving
Greed
Happiness
Harmony
Hatred
Information
Involvement
Learning
Love
Money
Notoriety
Order
Peace
Politics
Power
Praise
Prestige
Rebellion
Recognition

Redemption
Respect
Responsibility
Resolution
Retention
Revenge
Security
Self-improvement
Self-worth
Sharing
Simplicity
Status
Stress relief
Support
Time
Trust
Unity
Vanity
Victory
Vision

Needs and Priorities

Every motive we have for action arises from a need and our desire to satisfy it. When your body is hungry, it signals your brain, and you feel the need to eat. Your hunger creates a need to satisfy your discomfort by eating. If you ignore this feeling of hunger, it increases in strength until it overshadows any other motives that may have been taking precedence over it.

Motives come in many varieties and change throughout your lifetime. Consider a family vacation. Everyone is excited about going, but each individual has his or her own idea of fun. The parents are motivated by the opportunity to get away from work, the teenage son by the chance to meet girls at the beach, and the preteen daughter by the promise of a visit to the amusement park. They are all able to satisfy vastly different needs with the same tangible reward.

Motives can also change over the course of an activity. You may take up aerobics to lose weight and find that you actually enjoy the class. Soon, personal fulfillment becomes your primary motive and weight loss is a secondary benefit of your new hobby.

Actions Rewarded

In its most simplified form, motivation is based on motives and incentives. Motives are desires or needs that originate within you. Incentives are rewards that, when related to motives, become motivating. For example, if you want to lose weight, you might create the incentive of promising yourself new clothing when you can fit into a smaller size. If you like shopping and wearing new clothes, you may be highly motivated by this incentive. If you are not particularly fashion-oriented, this incentive probably would not motivate you.

To create a strong incentive, your reward for achieving a behavior must be directly tied to the motive for action. Your incentive also must be attractive enough for you to endure the required sacrifice to earn it. The excitement of reaching your goal and attaining its corresponding reward gives you endurance you might not otherwise have.

Choosing a Reward

When choosing an incentive bear in mind that people can respond differently to the same stimulus. Simply because a car dealership advertises big discounts on its new cars does not mean every person in town will hasten to the dealership to take advantage of the offer. Each potential customer must first have a corresponding motive - he or she must be at least remotely in need of a new car. A tantalizing reward alone does not motivate people to act. We are bombarded daily by hundreds of incentives to take action, yet react only to those for which we already have an underlying motive.

Often, the value of a reward is not in the reward itself, but in the emotional fulfillment that comes from receiving it. A child will happily do his chores to get smiley face stickers applied to his chore chart at the end of the day. The smiley faces themselves are insignificant, but the love and approval that they signify are invaluable.

Intrinsic vs. Extrinsic Reward

There are two classes of rewards that motivate people to act: intrinsic rewards and extrinsic rewards. Intrinsic rewards are the intangible feelings we have that motivate us like happiness, recognition, fulfillment, love, understanding, peace and acceptance. Intrinsic rewards are the most fulfilling and powerful for long-term motivation. They are also the most difficult to bring about because they require an active investment of emotional energy.

Extrinsic rewards are tangible materials that motivate us including money, awards, promotions, and gifts. Extrinsic rewards are easy to give and are powerful short-term motivators. The drawback is that they become addictive. Once you are motivated by an external reward for an action, you expect it the next time you perform the same action. And worse, as the novelty wears off, you may begin to expect more rewards for the same amount of effort.

Conditioned Response

Motivation is often the result of social conditioning and experience. Most adults are motivated to work for green paper (otherwise known as money) because they know it can be exchanged for material possessions that they value. The paper itself is not actually different from other paper, but we are conditioned to value money and learn to become motivated by it. If you want to test this theory, give a ten dollar bill to a one year old and she will probably rip it to pieces for the fun of it. Give it to a seven year old and she will be off to the toy store.

Motivation also can be negatively ingrained through experience. We tend to transfer experiences of failure from one area of our life to another. A young man who has experienced failure in successive jobs may be averse to going back to school for more training, assuming this too might fail. Although his lack of training might be the reason for his job failure, he resists getting the education he needs because he associates all work-related tasks with failure.

Motivation or Manipulation?

At times, the line between motivating and manipulating may seem to blur. When does the positive action of motivating become the negative action of manipulating? Manipulation is the act of deceiving someone into doing something he might not otherwise do. Motivation is the act of encouraging someone to do something he needs to do, but may not be able to initiate or complete on his own. When you motivate someone to do something, you build on his latent intrinsic desire to do it. When you manipulate a person into doing something, you create a false desire to do it.

As an example, imagine a baseball team. The coach of the team is aware that one of his average players has the potential to be a much better player, but is not applying himself to the game. Although the player is always on time for practice and follows instructions, he does not have the emotional commitment necessary to use his full potential. Of course he wants to play better, but he is not sure how to improve his game.

To motivate the player, the coach gives him a few performance goals to meet in practice, promising him a spot in the starting line-up if he can meet the goals within four weeks. This is an example of motivation. The player wants to improve and the coach provides him with the necessary direction and rewards to spur him on.

On the other hand, consider another team where the coach is not as caring and supportive. Instead, he has a personal vendetta against his star outfielder. They have never gotten along and the coach is anxious to be rid of him. The coach approaches an average player and mentions that if he works a little harder, he could have the star outfielder's position. He also mentions, deceitfully, that the star outfielder has made unkind remarks about the player behind his back.

This makes the second-string player angry and vindictive toward the star player. He begins to play little tricks on the star, hiding his equipment, making him late to practice, starting rumors about him, and generally distracting the outfielder from his game. When the star's performance becomes erratic, the coach seizes the opportunity to replace him with the second-string player, his intention from the beginning.

As you can see, manipulation is an unintelligent and negative form of motivation. Eventually, both players will figure out what the coach has done to them and turn against him. Consequently, manipulation is a very short-term answer. It might make the situation better for a short time after which things will get considerably worse.

Below is a list of motivating needs and actions (taken from the original list on page 11) that are usually manipulative, and therefore negative, motivators:

Anger
Betrayal
Control
Deception
Desperation
Ego
Fear
Greed
Money
Politics
Rebellion
Revenge
Vanity

When motivating yourself or others, it is best to avoid the motivators on the above list, since the results generally will be short-term and the problem will resurface when the initial motivation disappears. Consider a real life scenario in which the motivators are all negative. You work in a large manufacturing company and discover that a long-time rival has applied for a supervisory position in your department. Not wanting to see him advance ahead of you, you decide to apply for the position as well. Although you have little interest in the position, you are not particularly happy with your current job and do not want to be at the mercy of your contemptible colleague.

You are offered the job and accept it, but in a few weeks your rival finds a better job at another company and leaves your department. You suddenly realize that your job is no longer gratifying, now that your rival is not there to see your success. In fact, you now feel just as unhappy and empty as you did in your previous position. The reason? In short, your motives in applying for the new job were not related to your long-term success, rather to short-term vengeance against someone else. When your rival fled the scene, so did your motivation, leaving you with the same lamentable feelings with which you started.

Theories of Motivation

There are several accepted theories of motivation. While this book is not a scholarly text that subscribes to any one theory, understanding the background of motivation theory can help you apply the ideas presented in the following chapters.

The *Behavioral Theory*, probably the most commonly known motivational theory (everyone who has ever taken a high school psychology course is familiar with Pavlov's salivating dogs), states that desired behaviors recur when reinforced and that people can be influenced to behave like others whom they see rewarded for such behavior. According to the Behavioral Theory, one person can motivate another person simply by rewarding desirable behavior and punishing or ignoring undesirable behavior.

While we all know that this works for training pets, humans are more complicated. Humans have varied needs and desires and what one person perceives to be a reward may not have any effect on another. And there is always the risk that the desired behavior, once established, will disappear once the rewards cease.

The *Cognitive Theory* suggests that people are most motivated by things that pique their curiosity and are interesting or fun. This theory relies heavily on intrinsic motivation and the desire of the individual to answer a question, fulfill a need, or achieve competency in a subject. It does not, however, account for the reasons that people endure intense or prolonged suffering (neither interesting nor fun) to achieve a goal.

The ***Humanistic View*** is based on Abraham Maslow's idea that people have a fundamental drive to fulfill certain needs in a specific order. The basic human needs, according to the theory, are physiological satiation, safety, belonging, esteem, self-actualization, understanding, and aesthetic. As a level of need is quenched, a new level is approached and the quest to satisfy begins anew. Somewhat similarly, the ***Achievement Theory*** states that people develop a need for achievement and seek to fulfill that need while avoiding the possibility of failure.

While each theory has merits and applies in many real-life cases, a blanket theory to motivate people in every situation is elusive. The sheer number and complexity of variables involved in motivation defy a "perfect answer" or "magic technique". Motivation depends upon having an understanding of people and their wants and needs. Your ability to identify and fulfill these fundamental needs is the key to being a successful motivator.

Key Ideas

There are several key ideas that are essential to understanding motivation. For your reference, they are summarized below.

1. Motivation is a force, positive or negative that causes us to act.

2. Understanding the underlying motive behind the action is the key to motivating anyone, including yourself.

3. Every motive we have for action arises from a need and our desire to satisfy it.

4. Motives come in many forms and change throughout our lives.

5. Motives can change during an activity.

6. To create a strong incentive, your reward for achieving a behavior must be directly tied to the motive for action.

7. Motivation is often the result of social conditioning and experience.

8. Motivation is the act of encouraging someone to do something they need to do, but may not be able to initiate on their own. Manipulation is the act of deceiving someone into doing something they might not otherwise do.

Using this Book

"1,001 Ways to Motivate Yourself and Others" is divided into two major sections. The first seven chapters describe ways to motivate the different types of people in your life, including your peers, your boss, your employees, your clients, your team, your students, and most importantly, yourself. The remaining chapters describe ways to motivate yourself or others toward common actions that we often find difficult, including decision making, productivity, change, creativity, success, and leadership.

For ease of use, chapters are separated into *Inspiration* (ideas to spark you to action) and *Application* (specific ways to create motivation). When you know what you need to and are having trouble getting started, look for motivation in the *Inspiration* section. When you are ready to take action, but are not sure what you need to do, look for motivation in the *Application* section.

Part One

&

*Motivating
the People in
your Life*

Chapter Two

160 Ways to Motivate Yourself

160 Ways to Motivate Yourself

Knowing and doing are as different as night and day.

The gap between knowing and doing is where great men and women are made or lost. Most of us know what we have to do to achieve our dreams, but we have a hundred and one reasons not to act on our knowledge. We don't have enough money, we don't have enough time, we don't have the skills, we don't have the materials, we don't have the patience, we don't have the courage, and on and on into eternity.

The reality is that with all of the energy we use to think up and justify those excuses, we could be half way to achieving our goal. If only we had the motivation to get started on the "doing". That is where the first section of this book comes into play. The place we have to start practicing motivational skills is with ourselves. Once we can motivate ourselves, we can motivate anyone.

Now is the time to put all of your excuses to rest and start on the road to your dream. No matter what your excuse, you will find something in the passages that follow to counteract it. When you find the message that motivates you, write it down and carry it with you. When you find your excuses threatening your dream, take out your message and take heart in the knowledge that you can achieve your goal if you truly set your mind to it!

Inspiration

    ⁖   Failure is like driving down a dead end road and turning around to find a better route.

    ⁖   Winners don't have time to place blame, they're too busy getting ready for the next challenge.

    ⁖   Success is the greatest motivator.

    ⁖   It's better to try something great and fail, than to do nothing and succeed at it.

    ⁖   As long as you know where you are headed there is no need to justify it to others.

    ⁖   Everything ever accomplished in history was born of human thought and ingenuity.

    ⁖   Don't let who you are stunt who you want to be.

    ⁖   Conceive and believe to achieve.

    ⁖   Better to consider your route while you are on solid ground than to panic in the quicksand.

    ⁖   Sometimes how far you go is not as important as the direction you take.

    ⁖   Your goals must be clear but your guidelines must be flexible.

     Later never comes, there is only now.

     You can never live up to everyone's expectations, but you can live up to your own.

     Many people are talented yet few distinguish themselves. The ability to rise above lies more in effort than in talent.

     Everyone is good at something.

     Intentions don't count, actions do.

     There are many tasks in life that are unavoidable, whether you do them cheerfully or grudgingly is up to you.

     It is more fearful not to have a goal than not to reach a goal.

     What you are is more important than what you have been and what you aim to be is best of all.

     You cannot strike higher than you aim.

     Neither our greatest fears nor our greatest hopes are beyond the limits of our ability.

     If you don't know where you want to go, no amount of planning will get you there.

     Being able to do only a little is not an excuse for doing nothing at all.

      The ultimate motivator is defeat. When you hit bottom, you have nowhere to go but up.

      The motivation to succeed is much more valuable than knowledge or training. Motivation drives you to seek knowledge, but knowledge does not intrinsically create motivation.

      The future is where you will spend the rest of your life.

      Never risking the chance to make a mistake is the biggest mistake you can make.

      You are more likely to be motivated by the avoidance of adversity than by the attainment of peace.

      The joy of the journey is not so much in reaching the harbor as in anticipating what lies ahead.

      The only thing stopping you is yourself.

      To move your mind, set your body in motion.

      To move your body, first move your mind.

      There is no guarantee that tomorrow will come. Do it today.

      When your perception changes, the cloudy day turns sunny.

      Worry changes nothing but your mind.

     ⁎   Sages can point the way, but ultimately we must walk the road alone.

     ⁎   Nothing has control over your destiny but you.

     ⁎   Appreciate what you have.

     ⁎   Nothing is certain, so don't bet on it.

     ⁎   Impossible only means it will take a bit longer than planned.

     ⁎   The first step determines the direction of the journey.

     ⁎   Uninspiring goals produce uninspiring results.

     ⁎   There is no obstacle so great that it cannot be met head on or avoided.

     ⁎   Nothing makes life more mundane than habit.

     ⁎   Experience, whether good or bad, is an asset.

     ⁎   The rabbit outruns the fox because the fox is running for his dinner and the rabbit is running for his life.

     ⁎   No matter how bad your situation is, you always have the freedom to discover something good about yourself.

    ₧   You have to maximize what you have to get what you want.

    ₧   Doing leads to achieving. Being leads to becoming.

    ₧   Problems are teachers not obstacles.

    ₧   You are what you think you are.

    ₧   Potential - use it or lose it!

    ₧   What goes in strongly resembles what comes out.

    ₧   Where you start is not important, where you are going is.

    ₧   Adversity is the wrapping paper of opportunity.

    ₧   How you feel about your goals is more important than how others feel about them.

    ₧   What you do with your problem is more important than what your problem does with you.

    ₧   Allow yourself to dream, it just may come true.

    ₧   An obstacle is what you see when you stop focusing on your goal.

    ₧   The secret to good aim is having a big target.

    ₧   When the tide comes in, it lifts all things with it.

Application

   Make a habit of being enthusiastic.

   Don't forget to schedule play time.

   Find satisfaction in your daily life. Don't wait for your big break to come.

   Make a list of your 20 favorite things to do. How long has it been since you have done each? Neglecting your personal happiness is a powerful de-motivator.

   Be prepared - your opportunity may come at any moment.

   Surround yourself with positive, enthusiastic people.

   Create non-work situations, like sports and hobbies, where you can enjoy yourself and succeed.

   Do your best at every stage of the game.

   Ground yourself with solid principles so you don't get distracted from your goal by trends or fads.

   State your goals in the concrete instead of the intangible. Instead of saying "I want to be a rock star", quantify what it means to you to be a rock star like winning a grammy, getting a cover story in *Rolling Stone* or having a number one hit record.

      ⅎ   Be able to readily identify the most common de-motivators:

                                      a. fear of failure
                                        b. change in priorities
                                        c. uncertainty
                                        d. loneliness
                                        e. jealousy
                                        f. anger
                                        g. disappointment
                                        h. fear of the unknown

      ⅎ   Don't let yourself get trapped in other's negativity.

      ⅎ   When you can't get motivated, look at your situation as an objective observer, not a subjectively involved party.

      ⅎ   Don't let your weaknesses overshadow your strengths.

      ⅎ   Define the reasons behind your goals.

      ⅎ   Instead of saying "I can't reach my goal because I don't have X." think about what you can do to get X or how you can achieve your goal without X.

      ⅎ   There is only one person you must answer to in the end - yourself.

      ⅎ   Do what you love.

      ⅎ   Tackle small problems before they grow into unmanageable situations.

        When you face a daunting task, ask yourself "What can I do with what I have?"

        Set imminent goals and get started on them before your priorities change.

        When facing a difficult task or situation, acknowledge that you can neither be a perfect success nor a perfect failure. You will inevitably fall somewhere in-between.

        Cut out the unnecessary negatives in your life:
a. dwelling on bad news
b. accepting blame from others for their problems
c. being the target of nitpickers
d. being the target of chronically depressed friends
e. being the scapegoat for incompetent co-workers
f. being the target of chronically angry colleagues

        Avoid identifying too heavily with what you currently are, it blocks your progress toward something new.

        Focus on becoming.

        Don't get discouraged if it seems that nobody believes in you. Start a trend by believing in yourself.

        Replace the fantasy of what you could do with the reality of what you can do.

        Practice doing small, unpleasant tasks so when the time comes for real sacrifice, you are well trained.

ဆ   Love whatever you do.

ဆ   Identify the positives of a negative situation and cling to them tenaciously.

ဆ   You can have anything you want in life if you are willing to pay the price to achieve it.

ဆ   Always state your goals, dreams and aspirations in the first person, using "I" and "me" statements.

ဆ   Set specific goals. Instead of saying "I want to be happy" list the specific conditions that identify your attainment of happiness.

ဆ   Lighten up on yourself. Replace unrealistic personal rules like *"I have to be successful"*, *"I have to be perfect at work"* or *"I have to be a perfect husband"* with more realistic personal goals like *"I would like to do well at work and, although I can't control everything, I always make my best effort."*.

ဆ   Acknowledge that your destiny lies in your hands and you can make it or break it.

ဆ   Do it now.

ဆ   If you can't win at someone else's game, make your own game with rules you can succeed by.

ဆ   Always set a time limit on your goals.

- ✇   Change "if" to "when".

- ✇   Meaningful goals produce meaningful results.

- ✇   When something goes wrong, think constructively instead of imagining the worst. *Example: You are preparing a big presentation and your computer goes down. Instead of imagining the worst possible outcome (my presentation will fail, I will lose my job, I'll be fired), start thinking of concrete solutions (Whose computer can I borrow? How can I get an extension? What else can I use to make the presentation?).*

- ✇   An *I'll do it tomorrow* attitude brings *I should have done it yesterday* consequences.

- ✇   Never say never.

- ✇   See your goals happening in the present or near future, not "someday" or "later."

- ✇   It doesn't matter how many times you fall, only how many times you get up.

- ✇   Frame goals as positive action statements. Use *"I want to be healthier and more fit,"* not *"I don't want to be so fat."* Say *"I want to find a good job."* instead of *"I wish I could get rid of this lousy job."*

- ✇   Identify your procrastination habits. No one is free from habitual behaviors that obstruct motivation.

    ℬ   When you are depressed, try side-tracking your depression instead of eliminating it. Depression and sadness have a purpose and need to run their course, but they don't have to run your life. Put them on the back burner until they disappear naturally.

    ℬ   Be enthusiastic.

    ℬ   Meaningful goals are more likely to be reached than those that are set arbitrarily or by someone else.

    ℬ   Know the difference between considering problems and worrying about them. Consideration is productive, worry is futile.

    ℬ   Use positive language. Instead of saying *"I won't fail,"* say *"I will succeed."*

    ℬ   Never blame other people's actions for your lack of action. Anyone can try to make you angry, afraid or depressed, but your response to another person's actions will decide whether you are in control or being controlled.

    ℬ   Practice being motivated. You may fail at first, but practice makes perfect.

    ℬ   Accept failure as part of success.

    ℬ   Do nothing, you'll be amazed at how motivated you get when you deliberately try to stop all action.

ဢ   When you experience a serious setback, avoid comparing yourself to what you used to be or have. Instead, think about what you can have in the future. *Example: You just got fired. Instead of comparing how miserable you are now to how great it was to have a job, think about the possibilities that have opened up: a career change, going back to school, pursuing a dream, turning a hobby into a business, moving to a new city, etc.*

ဢ   Never give up.

ဢ   Be yourself without reservation.

ဢ   When you set goals, positively envision the specific steps you will take to accomplish them.

ဢ   Rather than viewing life as an endless string of problems to be solved, view it as an unfolding mystery to be revealed.

ဢ   See your dreams as a preview of the future.

ဢ   There is someone, somewhere who can help you. Find him or her.

ဢ   Use failure to spur you on to a better course of action.

ဢ   When minor failures occur, shift your focus to your big goal and assess the impact of the failure on the whole, not only on the area of the failure.

෮   Don't allow small annoyances to grow into pending
      emergencies.

෮   If you have trouble getting your work day started,
      choose the task you find most appealing and do it
      first every day. Choose something exciting or easy
      like opening mail, doing daily chores, checking
      e-mail, returning messages, etc. This will put you
      in a positive mindset to start the day.

෮   Set aside time everyday for yourself.

෮   Have a goal for every day, even if it is to do
      nothing.

෮   Ask yourself "Am I better at ____ today than I was
      yesterday?" If you cannot say "yes" today, do some-
      thing about it so you can say "yes" tomorrow.

෮   Do something nice for someone else.

෮   Be committed.

෮   To cause a specific feeling, assume the physical
      position you associate with it. *Example: If you are
      about to make a public speech and want to feel
      confident; stand straight, practice your facial
      expressions and hand gestures, etc.*

෮   Tackle difficult or unpleasant tasks immediately after
      you experience success.

෮   Take time to enjoy and congratulate yourself for
      progress.

ℴ   Feed your mind and your soul.

ℴ   The best way to make a commitment to a course of action is to begin with a productive step, no matter how small.

ℴ   Avoid comparing yourself to others.

ℴ   When assessing your achievements, compare yourself to your past self or your potential.

ℴ   Choose quality over quantity.

ℴ   The difference between good and great is related to how much you care about what you are doing.

ℴ   Don't settle for less than your best.

ℴ   Don't give too much credit to other people's negative opinions about your goals.

ℴ   Get involved. And care about the people you get involved with.

ℴ   Remove de-motivating factors from your environment. Take the couch out of your office, unplug the TV., put away the tabloids.

ℴ   You have to start somewhere, and there is no better time or place than here and now.

Chapter Three

60 Ways to Motivate your Boss

60 Ways to Motivate Your Boss

Credentials are easily replaceable, commitment and integrity are not.

If you have a boss or employer, then you know the advantages of being liked and respected by him or her. When your boss sees you in a favorable light, it is easier to do your job and easier to get ahead doing it. If your boss does not respect your efforts or judgment, your job is not only more difficult to do, but it becomes increasingly unpleasant with every passing day.

Motivating your boss means giving your boss reason to let you do your job the way you work best and giving you the chance to advance your career. To get your boss on your side, you have to supply irreplaceable qualities like sincerity, loyalty, commitment, integrity, and perseverance. If you are putting all your motivational skills to work, your boss may find dozens of people with the skills and credentials to fill your job, but no one who can truly replace you.

Inspiration

- ☐   If you cost your boss more than you earn for her, you won't be around very long.

- ☐   It's not enough to get things done, you should be seen doing them.

- ☐   Knowledge is power. Share it with your boss and your influence will increase measurably.

- ☐   You are less likely to have to work for a grumpy boss if you make a conscious effort to avoid doing things that make him grumpy.

- ☐   You don't have to like your boss but you should respect him.

- ☐   The threat of removing a motivating force can be also be highly motivating.

- ☐   Positive expectations usually lead to positive outcomes.

- ☐   Everyone wants something in life. Do you know what makes your boss tick?

- ☐   Give and you shall receive.

- ☐   Ask and you may receive.

- ☐   A win-win situation is the ideal motivator.

Application

📁   If you want your boss to back up your new ideas, be willing to share the credit.

📁   Stay informed about the important decisions your boss needs to make and discreetly provide her with helpful information from the front lines.

📁   Make your boss' weaknesses your strengths and offer assistance. You will become indispensable.

📁   The five most serious de-motivators for employers are an employee who is:
>   a. disloyal
>   b. out of control
>   c. insubordinate, especially in public
>   d. impudent
>   e. gunning for his boss's job

📁   Your boss is not responsible for your personal problems - leave them at home where they belong.

📁   Be prepared to show that you have exhausted your resources before asking your boss for help.

📁   Present new ideas in well thought-out, brief proposals that show both the positive and negative sides, so your boss doesn't run into surprises when she presents the idea to her superiors.

📁   Never steal your boss's spotlight or beat her at her game.

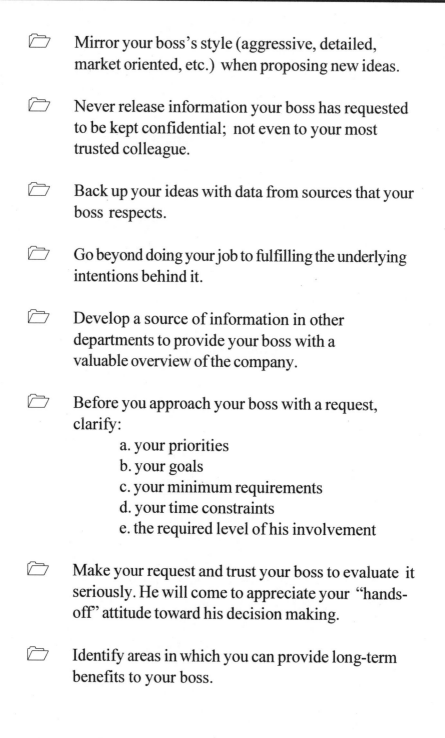

Mirror your boss's style (aggressive, detailed, market oriented, etc.) when proposing new ideas.

Never release information your boss has requested to be kept confidential; not even to your most trusted colleague.

Back up your ideas with data from sources that your boss respects.

Go beyond doing your job to fulfilling the underlying intentions behind it.

Develop a source of information in other departments to provide your boss with a valuable overview of the company.

Before you approach your boss with a request, clarify:
  a. your priorities
  b. your goals
  c. your minimum requirements
  d. your time constraints
  e. the required level of his involvement

Make your request and trust your boss to evaluate it seriously. He will come to appreciate your "hands-off" attitude toward his decision making.

Identify areas in which you can provide long-term benefits to your boss.

☞ Give more than you have to. Don't be on time, be early. Don't meet requirements, exceed them.

☞ Always present the mutual benefits of your proposal to open your boss's mind favorably to your ideas.

☞ Publicly praise your boss when you sincerely see an opportunity to do so.

☞ Don't expect your boss to be perfect. Accept his errors graciously and he is likely to do the same for you.

☞ Avoid surprises. Your boss will look forward to working with you if he knows you are honest.

☞ Never disparage your boss in front of your subordinates.

☞ Treat your boss with the same consideration you give your best customer or client.

☞ Go with the flow.

☞ Be willing to accept partial success for your projects and build on it. Your boss will see you as committed and mature.

☞ Give your boss confidence in your ability to do the necessary background research that will make both of you look good.

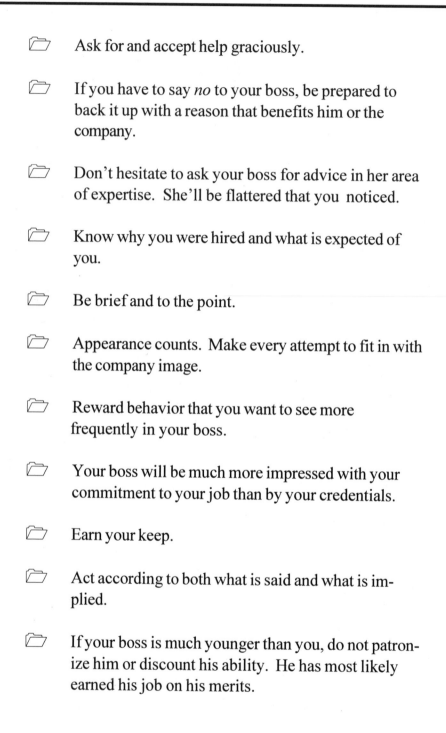

📁   Ask for and accept help graciously.

📁   If you have to say *no* to your boss, be prepared to back it up with a reason that benefits him or the company.

📁   Don't hesitate to ask your boss for advice in her area of expertise. She'll be flattered that you noticed.

📁   Know why you were hired and what is expected of you.

📁   Be brief and to the point.

📁   Appearance counts. Make every attempt to fit in with the company image.

📁   Reward behavior that you want to see more frequently in your boss.

📁   Your boss will be much more impressed with your commitment to your job than by your credentials.

📁   Earn your keep.

📁   Act according to both what is said and what is implied.

📁   If your boss is much younger than you, do not patronize him or discount his ability. He has most likely earned his job on his merits.

☞   Help your boss stay organized and on top of her
       work.

☞   Offer to "run interference" in situations that make
       your boss uncomfortable.

☞   Listen more than you talk.

Chapter Four

111 Ways to Motivate your Employees

111 Ways to Motivate your Employees

If money were such a great motivator, we would all be bank robbers.

Employers who think they can motivate employees with money alone face a stark wake-up call when all is said and done. Believe it or not, you cannot buy good help, you have to earn it. Of course, you can buy average or adequate employees, but that will not help you get ahead in today's business climate. If you want to succeed, or even keep up, you have to be above average in every contact with your customers.

Above average employees are motivated by the potential to be a part of something great, to make a difference, to contribute their share, to shine. You can motivate your employees to turn in stellar performances by giving them not only the opportunity to shine, but also the tools and knowledge to take advantage of that opportunity.

Inspiration

+ When you don't care, they don't care.

+ Employees feel secure, and therefore work best, when they trust their boss.

+ Successful motivation consists not of doing it to people but doing it with them.

+ You get from people exactly what you expect to get.

+ The best way to develop respect and responsibility in employees is to give it to them.

+ A balance of praise, criticism and silence makes your actions most sincere.

+ Lead by example.

+ Motivation is rarely self-sustaining; it must be re-ignited regularly.

+ Employees are most highly motivated when they feel they are appropriately compensated for what they produce.

+ Those who play well together work well together.

+ Those who work well together, work smarter.

✦   Neither the human mind nor the power to motivate it are strictly logical.

✦   Simplify.

✦   When the work and the worker fit, there is no need for further motivation.

✦   Criticism is most effective for getting back on track, not for getting started.

✦   Too many rules impede morale.

✦   Making requests is generally preferable to giving orders.

✦   A major determinant of job satisfaction is the relationship that employees have with one another.

✦   Always give credit where credit is due.

✦   Intrinsic satisfaction (competence, achievement, pride, personal growth) is the best motivator.

✦   The power of persuasion is longer lasting and more effective than the power of intimidation.

✦   The size of the reward should fit the size of the task.

Application

✦   New or less skilled employees are motivated most effectively by specific instruction and skill oriented tasks.

✦   Treat others as you want to be treated.

✦   Praise employees most frequently in areas of their work that they take most seriously.

✦   Create a workplace that is free of prejudice.

✦   Seasoned or highly skilled employees are highly motivated by a framework of general support and guidance within which they can create their own work style.

✦   Be generous with small mistakes and your employees will know you mean business when you correct or discipline them.

✦   When an employee's salary meets his needs, a raise (especially a modest one) is not a particularly strong motivator.

✦   Know how to express yourself in a variety of ways. Not every employee will respond to your personal style of communication.

✦   Respect your employees' need for confidentiality.

✦   Set firm rules and enforce them without exception.

✦   Give each of your workers a special, personal mission.

✦   Don't get involved in employees' personality conflicts.

✦   When faced with a company-wide project, create two teams. Establish their time and quality goals, then watch as they strive to better each other.

✦   Company policy must be consistent through all levels. Don't ask production employees to take pay cuts while senior executives get more perks.

✦   For a job exceptionally well done, send a letter to your boss (with a copy to the employee involved) extolling the employee's outstanding contribution to the company.

✦   Motivate competent employees by:

   a. giving them the freedom to choose how to organize their work
   b. creating a consensus on company goals
   c. avoiding micro-management of their daily work
   d. allowing them to participate in decision making
   e. identifying their "niche" in the company
   f. encouraging innovation

✦   Apologize honestly for your mistakes.

✦   Let talented employees feel they have the power to make a difference.

✦   Teach employees how to serve customers without feeling subservient.

✦   Never assign two people to do the job of one, it promotes boredom, frustration, and apathy.

✦   Periodically review your consistency in application of the rules. Inconsistency breeds contempt and encourages attempts to avoid the rules.

✦   Provide time for employees to pursue special interest projects that may result in new areas of development for the company.

✦   Make sure all employees take regular vacations to renew their spirit.

✦   Avoid the latest leadership and management fads.

✦   Visualize your ideal company and share your vision with your employees.

✦   Regularly check that the equipment your employees use to do their job works properly. Equipment in good working order prevents delays and supports quality work.

✦   Reward the right activities and discourage the wrong ones. This sounds simple but is too often disregarded.

✦   One of the biggest de-motivators for employees is

being asked to go down with a sinking ship.

✦ When an employee's suggestion saves the company money or boosts profits, let the employee share in the rewards.

✦ Set your "positive feedback quota" for the day. Consciously resolve to find a minimum of one good thing to say about each employee.

✦ Never delegate without a clear direction in mind. Communicate your goals and expectations clearly.

✦ Don't use employees as scapegoats for your mistakes.

✦ Treat employees like responsible adults.

✦ Make the upgrades and enhancements to equipment that help your employees do their job better.

✦ Help employees relate to what they produce by taking them out to the field to see their work "at work."

✦ Create indirect motivation through:

a. making your work atmosphere highly energetic
b. creating harmony among workers
c. encouraging friendly competition
d. simplifying ideas
e. developing role models
f. fostering team spirit

✦   Provide opportunities for personal skill development and advancement for self-enrichment.

✦   Make the chain of command clear and follow it strictly.

✦   Create the feeling of being part of something special, not just going to work every day.

✦   Listen to employee suggestions and requests regarding equipment upgrades, changes, and improvements.

✦   Show a willingness to try out employee ideas and innovations.

✦   Always preserve some mystery to heighten expectations.

✦   Create links between company goals and personal goals.

✦   Reward results over busy work.

✦   Have more patience with your employees than with yourself.

✦   Raise morale by allowing employees to design or decorate their work space. They know better than you how they work best.

✦   Never take sides among employees.

✦   Reward dependability as often as you reward innovation.

✦   Never criticize people for asking questions, seeking more information or requesting clarification.

✦   Do not tolerate rumors or gossip.

✦   Give your employees a vision to strive for.

✦   When morale is low because of another manager's style or criticism, provide enough hands-on direction to help complete the task as well as plenty of moral support when it is finished to restore employee confidence.

✦   Praise progress as well as results.

✦   Show an interest in employees as people and as workers.

✦   Don't be afraid to criticize.

✦   Create a system that allows employees to submit ideas to management.

✦   Don't wait to say thank you or show appreciation. When you see a job well done, immediately let the "doer" know how you feel about it.

✦   For major projects, set intermediate goals and rewards.

✦   Know your employees' likes and dislikes.

✦   Create a club for high achievers/producers.

✦   For experienced employees who are losing interest or getting side-tracked, inject a shot of pointed criticism.

✦   Help successful employees gain publicity in local news or national trade magazines.

✦   Never take credit for employees' work.

✦   Never abuse your power.

✦   Announce changes in advance and prepare employees to implement them smoothly.

✦   Bright but insecure employees need support to draw out their contributions. Help them refine their ideas in private before presenting them to the larger group. Support them and build a consensus around their ideas at presentation time.

✦   Have faith in your employees' ability to do their jobs.

✦   Develop strong relationships with subordinates who have influence among your staff.

✦   Create an employee of the month award and display it publicly.

✦   When an employee has minimal skills but great potential, take a hands-on approach until he becomes self-directed.

✦   Avoid criticizing new employees until they know
      your standards and expectations.

✦   Show confidence in your employees and give them
      reason to do the same.

✦   Distribute information through the proper channels.
      Never cut anyone out of the information loop.

✦   Measure and track key statistics. People do best in
      areas they know you are tracking regularly.

✦   Never reward an employee for doing less than was
      originally agreed upon.

✦   Treat your employees the way you want them to treat
      your customers.

✦   Always have at least one person on your staff who
      will tell you the truth no matter what.

✦   Grant rewards sporadically.

Chapter Five

75 Ways to Motivate your Team

75 Ways to Motivate your Team

Don't trod on the process to reach the goal.

I am sure many of you are thinking that this section is irrelevant to you. You do not coach a major league baseball team or a professional football team or even little league. But perhaps you have been in charge of a fund raising drive, a sales drive, a PTO committee, a research project or a marathon organizing committee. Teams come in many different forms and are not confined to the world of sports.

Any group of people striving towards a common goal work best when motivated as a team. Team spirit, camaraderie, goal setting and pulling together in the last dash for the finish line are all powerful group motivators. In fact, the feelings we get as part of a team are more powerful motivators than actually reaching the goal itself. The satisfaction of a job well done or a best effort is more lasting than any prize or trophy. Encourage your team to enjoy the process and watch as they run headlong into their goal on the way.

Inspiration

❖   Competition is only motivating if there is a prospect of winning.

❖   Teams are made of team players not superstars.

❖   Those who work well together play well together.

❖   The rewards of success must be shared equally among all team members whatever their level of contribution.

❖   Your team will give you what they think you expect from them.

❖   Know where your team is headed and be willing to meet them half way.

❖   People respond best when they can make the best use of their talents.

❖   Do it with your team rather than to them.

❖   As a team leader, your approach is a stronger motivator than your methods.

❖   Knowing when to use your authority is as important as knowing how to use it.

❖   Intrinsic fulfillment is the best long-term motivator.

❖   Insurmountable challenges are instant de-motivators.

❖   Discipline allows people to act in concert based on common principles.

Application

❖   Don't make promises or threats you don't intend to keep.

❖   Get everyone motivated by getting everyone involved. Not everyone can be a star player, but they can have a say in choosing team colors, selecting mascots, thinking of nicknames, leading cheers, keeping stats, designing plays, etc. Everyone is enthusiastic when they see their ideas as part of the whole.

❖   Create an atmosphere in which individual team members are willing to make personal sacrifices for the good of the team.

❖   Have a team mission that is the basis of the team's actions. *Example:* To win the league championship, to make the most sales in region A, to raise the most corporate donations.

❖   Use humor to dissolve interpersonal tension among team members.

❖   If your team enjoys the process, the goal becomes secondary and motivation becomes intrinsic.

❖   Don't ask your team to fight marginally important battles - they squander valuable morale and resources with little benefit.

❖   Expect team members to resolve differences, even if they cannot be entirely compatible.

❖   Participate in non-competitive activities as a team: march in a parade, go to a professional ball game, attend a clinic or seminar, hold a car wash, rake leaves for the elderly, etc.

❖   Foster group cohesiveness by ensuring that:

a. everyone works equally hard
b. everyone is willing to give their best for the good of the team
c. everyone hears about good news (news reports about the team, records set, awards earned)
d. there is active two way communication
e. there is a conflict resolution system in place
f. discipline is applied equitably and consistently

❖   Every team member should have a task suited to his talents. Don't ask a pitcher to play the outfield.

❖   Squelch rebels and dissenters before they take the team morale down with them.

and hobbies. Everyone should be discouraged from obsessing on a single pursuit.

❖ Encourage team members to participate voluntarily in all team events for the benefit of the team.

❖ Never stop teaching your team new and better winning skills.

❖ Talk with other successful team motivators. Study their style as well as their advice.

❖ Distribute written team rules and enforce them without bias.

❖ Push team members to their full potential but never forget to respect their dignity.

❖ Invite successful people in the field to instruct or talk to your team. Ask them to give an "I did it and so can you." message.

❖ In bad times, encourage team members to stick together for moral support.

❖ Develop team spirit by finding something for your team to specialize in. Example: hardest working, most home runs, best spirit, best defense, most eclectic, etc. Use your specialty to create team pride and build team spirit.

❖ Don't reward outstanding team members at the expense of others.

❖ Have a written *bill of rights* for team members

❖   Have a written *bill of rights* for team members defining the rights and responsibilities of being a part of the team.

❖   Team motivation is significantly increased when:

   a. members perceive that progress is being made
   b. members trust their leader
   c. team participation is perceived as interesting and
      meaningful
   d. members are rewarded for their efforts
   e. members take pride in their efforts
   f. members have mutual respect

❖   Point out errors without placing blame.

❖   Recognize increased effort, intensity, or persistence in less talented team members.

❖   Videotape your team at work and allow them to critique their performance. A video points out errors and highlights areas of excellence.

❖   With a team of strong personalities, harmony may seem impossible. Set a goal for everyone to reach their personal best performance through managed competition. *Example*: On an all-star team, time together is short and talent is plentiful. Instead of seeking team harmony, set a goal for everyone to break a personal record such as most hits in a game or most plays without an error.

❖   Create a team identity with team names, mascots, slogans, colors, cheers, etc.

❖ Insist on tolerance of individual traits within the group.

❖ Help your team identify with the achievements and goals of its parent organization such as the Little League, Boy's Club, Girl Scouts, etc. Make the team feel like part of the big picture.

❖ Avoid stereotyping young team members, especially from year to year. Youngsters are in a constant state of change. You must recognize and reward their efforts to improve themselves.

❖ Be able to identify common signs that team spirit is faltering:

  a. many team members are lazy
  b. team members avoid any responsibilities that do not directly affect them
  c. infighting among teammates or groups of members
  d. lack of self-respect
  e. lack of intrinsic satisfaction
  f. frequent conflicts among team members

❖ Give team members occasional opportunities to lead small group activities in practice to identify potential future leaders and encourage leadership.

❖ Create an atmosphere of support in which all team members cheer each other on.

❖ Avoid sacrificing individual contributions for team welfare.

❖   Team members are more likely to contribute when they feel that their contribution is identifiable. Create a system that clearly designates and recognizes individual effort.

❖   If everyone gives their best level of effort, though the results may not be spectacular, they deserve to participate in the rewards .

❖   Use team leaders to create positive emotional and mental trends among team members.

❖   Make it difficult for individuals to blend into the background.

❖   Use peer review to provide team members with constructive criticism from teammates.

❖   Avoid pitting teammates against each other to increase individual performance. Each member may invest more energy in bringing down the others than in improving himself.

❖   Establish team and individual goals simultaneously to create cohesion between the two.

❖   Give special tasks to substitutes, stand-ins and second-string players so they don't feel left out.

❖   Reward effort in preparatory work as consistently as you reward effort in the main event.

Chapter Six

54 Ways to Motivate your Students

54 Ways to Motivate your Students

Models leave longer lasting impressions than critics.

The teacher, like the team leader, is a role that often comes in disguise. You may not teach in school, but certainly you occasionally have the opportunity to pass along your knowledge of something to others. Perhaps you train new employees at your job or teach others a favorite hobby or sport. We all find ourselves sharing our knowledge with others from time to time, whether in a formal classroom setting or a more informal exchange of ideas.

Teaching can be one of the most frustrating tasks you can undertake. Although you can easily perform a skill yourself, you may find yourself perplexed when you try to get someone else to do it correctly. No matter how you explain it, they just cannot see it your way and you begin to wonder if it wouldn't just be easier to do it yourself. This is a critical juncture in motivating your student to succeed. If you give up and berate the student (colleague, employee, ...) you will alienate him and block any further progress.

However, if you draw on your motivational skills to provide a good role model and plenty of encouragement interspersed with meaningful guidance, you may be surprised at the sudden turnaround in your student's learning.

Inspiration

- Students are eager to learn skills that give them control over their environment.

- Students like to learn skills that help them gain social acceptance.

- Intellectual wonder is a powerful motivator in learning.

- When students learn a new subject, they prefer to practice on specific tasks they can master easily.

- Insurmountable challenges extinguish even the brightest burning motivation.

- If you are not motivated, you cannot expect your students to understand the value of motivation.

- As soon as a student is presented with new material, she forms an opinion about it. If this opinion is not positive, everything that follows is diminished.

- Students are motivated primarily through curiosity or fear, with curiosity being the stronger of the two.

- Students must believe that their goals are attainable and meaningful.

- Your students' behavior is a direct response to how you treat them.

▤   The presentation of new material creates three
possible responses:
     1. instant adaptation
     2. frustration and resignation
     3. coping with frustration and trying to adapt
Prepare for every contingency in advance.

▤   Never blame your students for a lack of motivation.
You must make more effort.

Application

▤   Make learning progressive and point out progress as
it occurs.

▤   In the early stages of learning, recognize effort above
results.

▤   If your students easily accomplish everything you
teach them, your standards are too low.

▤   Make it hard for students to blend into the
background. Require everyone to make quality
contributions regularly.

▤   Criticize the behavior, not the behave-er.

▤   Make learning fun through role playing and
educational games.

- Motivate students to think and participate by asking open-ended questions. *Example*: Instead of asking "*Any questions?*", ask "*What questions do you have?*"

- Praise progress as well as results.

- Select goals and rewards that are tied directly to student needs. *Example:* A woman signs up for a shooting course to learn self-protection. Setting goals related to basic proficiency and safety are more important to her than proper breathing techniques or learning to handle an exotic variety of weapons.

- Whenever possible use "hands on " methods to teach new concepts and skills.

- Make every effort to reduce the potential for failure or fear of failure associated with learning.

- Give students clear criteria that identify when they have reached their goal.

- Call attention to things done right rather than errors. Build successful habits around these positive things.

- Select a "student of the month" or similar award.

- Adult students have established value systems and habits. Present ideas and let adult students accept them at their own pace.

- Students prefer learning from teachers who are well rounded and interesting. They subconsciously believe that the knowledge presented by the teacher is what led him to become so interesting and they want to acquire that knowledge.

- Simplify tasks and directions to avoid confusion.

- Provide time for students to interact with people who have already reached similar goals similar to those that your students have chosen.

- Never threaten students with punishment or consequences you can't or don't intend to carry out.

- Take time out to show students how they can apply their knowledge in "the real world."

- Give top students the opportunity to apply their skills by tutoring slower students.

- Students are most highly motivated to learn when they believe you can help them or offer them something of value.

- Make it clear what you expect to be done and what the results of doing it will be.

- Give talented students the chance to participate in workshops, clinics, projects, independent study and other activities that challenge them to apply their knowledge.

- Use familiar ideas (through allegories or anecdotes) to introduce complex or new ideas.

- Give constructive criticism without placing blame for failure or errors.

- Establish a team atmosphere in which stronger students are encouraged to help others meet classroom goals and standards as a group.

- Use peer review to encourage critical thinking and provide students with several viewpoints about their work.

- Reward self-initiated learning.

- Show students that you recognize the difference between productive work and "busy work."

- When you can't answer a question, admit it and agree to find the answer. Your students will respect your candor and self-assuredness.

- Give students the chance to personalize the classroom with artwork and meaningful personal possessions.

- Establish a minimum number of times per day that you will give positive feedback and actively look for opportunities to meet your quota.

▤   Implement students' suggestions where feasible and see that they get appropriate credit.

▤   When you give rewards, make sure the size of the reward fits the size of the task.

▤   Create teams to work on large projects to provide moral support and reduce the burden of work on any one person.

▤   Maintain and enforce consistent classroom rules.

▤   When a student reaches a learning plateau, go back to more familiar material to restore her confidence and recreate a successful mindset.

▤   Adults make self-conscious students. Acknowledge their concerns at the outset.

Chapter Seven

56 Ways
to Motivate
your Peers

56 Ways to Motivate your Peers

Persuasion is the best form of motivation when appealing to those you have no authority over.

Some of the most difficult people to motivate are your colleagues and associates. They are parallel in stature to you and therefore not compelled to take orders from you. They also see little to gain by associating with someone whom they perceive to be no more influential than they are. In short, why should they bother to do you any favors when they could be impressing someone who has real influence?

The key to motivating your peers is to convince them that you have something they need and that you are willing to share it with them - if they will provide you with something of equal value. Although you may not have the power or influence that they are looking for, you have many more things to offer your colleagues including cooperation, trust, resources, alliances, information, and status. Take stock of what you have to offer and what your colleagues need. Then persuade them to meet you half way.

Inspiration

 ↾ The bottom line is that everyone wants to fulfill his needs.

 ↾ You cannot motivate influential people unless you are motivated.

 ↾ A good talker is perceived as influential; a good listener as sage.

 ↾ Never put all of your cards on the table at once.

 ↾ Great ideas attract great minds.

 ↾ You don't have to like people to work with them.

 ↾ Your peers will reflect your motivation style, positive or negative, back on you.

 ↾ A reputation for getting the job done consistently and reliably attracts quality people into your sphere of influence.

 ↾ If you don't know your colleague's position, assuming she is an ally will get you off to a better start than assuming she is an adversary.

 ↾ Having access to information or control over resources gives you significant influence over your peers.

- ❧ Lead with style and follow up with substance.

- ❧ Requesting or encouraging will get you a lot farther than demanding or pleading.

- ❧ You can achieve the most when you don't care who gets the credit.

Application

- ❧ Create empathy among your peers by relating your personal needs in an emotionally meaningful way.

- ❧ Show your willingness to do your share.

- ❧ Be able to show that you have put forth your best effort before asking a colleague for assistance.

- ❧ Conceal your intentions so people are compelled to watch and wonder about what they might be.

- ❧ Your associates are more likely to go along with your idea if they think they thought of the idea first.

- ❧ Peers are often reluctant to make the first move for fear of rejection. By taking the first step in a business relationship, you motivate your peers to meet you half way.

❧   Let your associates know that their help is essential.

❧   Appeal to your peers' self-importance.

❧   When you create an image of being strong,
       powerful or influential, you are more likely to
       be treated as such by others. How to create such
       an image? Act as if it already exists!

❧   Fighting for an issue is admirable, but knowing when
       to cut your losses is essential to avoid being branded
       a "lost cause".

❧   If you are younger than most of your co-workers,
       emphasize your experience and willingness to accept
       challenges.

❧   If you cannot motivate your peers to support you, at
       least motivate them not to support your enemies.

❧   Praise your colleagues for success in the areas they
       value most. They'll be immensely glad you noticed.

❧   Be prepared to offer your colleague something he
       needs or wants, as opposed to whatever you can
       afford to spare.

❧   Be willing to swallow personal differences in favor
       of a working professional relationship.

❧   Show your associate what a difference his help can
       make.

- Ask for advice, it makes people feel helpful and smart.

- Encourage associates to depend on you, rather than to get what they want and move on.

- Be a problem solver.

- Talk less. Listen more.

- Seek long-term cooperative agreements over one shot deals.

- Give your peers a vision of a better tomorrow if they align themselves with you.

- Don't get involved in a colleague's business when it doesn't concern you.

- Don't be afraid to sacrifice recognition occasionally to get the job done. If you are consistently associated with getting things done, people will notice.

- Never ask someone to do something you can do for yourself.

- Give your peers reason to both like and trust you.

- When faced with a difficult colleague, try doing the opposite of what he expects to put him off guard and open his mind to your ideas. Then let your seriousness and sincerity win him over.

- Avoid being on the losing side too often.

- Show your trust by not going behind the backs of colleagues for information.

- If you know you cannot win, concede grudgingly, making it clear that you don't agree but will make a concession for the good of the cause. You will, at the very least, build goodwill.

- Avoid burning bridges you may have to recross in the future.

- Do someone a favor without expecting an immediate payback. Eventually you will have reason to call in the favor.

- Be a team player.

- Be discreet with confidences revealed by a colleague.

- When you cannot rely on authority to lead a group, use coalition building skills to motivate others to interact and follow your lead.

- Resist forming first impressions based on emotion.

- Don't waste your associate's valuable time.

- Take the time to really listen to other people's needs.

- Recognize that the people who really get things done are often difficult to work with. Rather than avoiding these personality types in your business life, learn to accept them for that they are and channel their positive qualities into getting the job done.

- Be *for* things instead of *against* their opposites. *Example*: Instead of being against the school budget, be for quality education.

- Introduce two people who have something in common. If they benefit, they will both feel obliged to repay the favor.

- Give as much attention to well established relation-ships as you give to budding alliances.

Chapter Eight

50 Ways to Motivate your Clients and Customers

50 Ways to Motivate your Clients and Customers

Customers respond to kindness by coming back for more.

The bottom line in dealing with customers or clients is that if they are happy, they will come back and if they are not, they can get what they need elsewhere. Your customers are most happy when you can fulfill their needs and solve their problems efficiently, pleasantly and at a price that doesn't break their budget. Everything else is just the icing on the cake.

Inspiration

In the long run, honesty really is the best policy.

Clients want results, not products. They want reliable transportation, clean clothes, a cozy home - not a new car, a new washing machine or a new house. The feeling a possession brings is more powerful than the possession itself.

Hospitality is a welcome change in our frenzied life.

Why you do things and the way you do them, is more important than what you do.

People are more likely to buy from you if they feel you understand their needs, than if they understand the features of your product or service.

Know the difference between simply treating people well and making them feel important.

A smile is the universal language.

Customers are more likely to bring repeat business if they feel they are more than just money in your pocket.

Favor relationships over transactions.

- Customers prefer that you provide quality goods or services the first time, but if you cannot, they expect you to deliver on your original promise without delay.

- People like to have the newest and the best, but they don't necessarily want to be the first to have it.

- Meeting customer expectations is more important than your objective level of quality. People expect fast food at a fast food restaurant and gourmet food at a gourmet restaurant. You don't have to be a gourmet to run a fast food joint.

- People like to do business with people they like.

Application

- Prove your commitment to excellence through your daily actions.

- If your client is a socializer, don't rush into your business pitch. Take time to socialize first.

- If your client is a busy person, get right to the point. Busy people are used to making quick decisions and don't like to be "sold".

- Reward clients for choosing you by providing exceptional service, attention to detail and consistency.

- Take the opportunity to personalize interactions (letters, meetings, phone calls) with clients whenever possible.

- Be your own best customer. *Example:* A fitness trainer should be lean and muscular, a make-up saleswoman should wear make-up well, a car salesman should drive the car he sells.

- Exceed expectations.

- Follow up often and sincerely.

- Help your clients defeat their enemies, real or perceived.

- To motivate customers to buy, offer to "fulfill their needs" rather than by "selling" them something.

- Believe in your product.

- Remind your customers of the great deals and service they get when they do business with you. Giving them great deals is not enough if they do not consciously acknowledge their value.

- Always keep your promises.

Keep customers happy even after you've finished your business with them.

Be willing to let your client shine in the spotlight while you stand in the shadow.

Resolve problems quickly and with style. Clients keep coming back if they trust you to deal with complaints about your products or service.

Clients like consistency.

Be willing to lose a sale today to preserve a long-term relationship with a client.

Provide customers with the opportunity to feel they have made a good decision.

Treat clients like lifetime partners in your business.

Take the boredom, drudgery or fear out of using your product or service. Every industry has a downside. Acknowledge yours and let your customers know exactly what you will do about it.

When a customer is undecided, present two options and the basis for choosing each to motivate him to make a decision.

Don't let a problem with a previous customer affect your interaction with the next customer.

Make a "customer's bill of rights" for all employees to follow. Every employee should:
- a. be on time
- b. acknowledge a customer's presence, even when busy
- c. keep appointments
- d. understand products and services
- e. listen carefully to customers
- f. be straight forward
- g. honestly admit when they cannot provide what a customer wants

Make your client's primary objective your primary objective.

Offer customers enough choices, in terms of price and quality, so everyone can find an appropriate option.

Be a good citizen and let your customers know about your contributions to the community.

Motivation does not have to cost money. Even something as small as an extra button for a shirt is really appreciated when the customer uses it.

Deliver on special requests, special orders, and personalized service whenever possible.

View a sale as the conclusion to one part of your relationship with the customer and the beginning of another part.

Part Two

&

Motivating to Overcome Barriers

Chapter Nine

75 Ways
to
Motivate
Change

75 Ways to Motivate Change

The best time to change is before you are forced to.

Change is one of the most frequently recurring, yet one of the most frightening aspects of human life. The very act of living subjects us to ongoing change, both within and around us. Change is a reality that cannot be avoided or ignored - much as some of us might try.

The best way to motivate yourself to change is to enthusiastically meet the change head on before it is forced upon you. Avoiding an impending change, especially a major one, is a primary source of stress, anxiety, and physical illness. Change is often unpleasant or uncertain. Having to face the unpleasant or the uncertain is best done in a positive state of mind, rather than when you are anxious or ill. The next time you face a major change, resolve to use all of your motivational skills to deal with it head on, whatever the consequences.

Motivate Yourself

⊠ Recognize self-defeating excuses and refuse to listen to them.

⊠ Never fear change.

⊠ When you begin something new, expect to be horrible at it. This makes the inevitable mistakes easier to swallow.

⊠ To initiate a change, start with a step that will bring noticeable results, no matter how small.

⊠ Nothing in life leaves you where it finds you.

⊠ Minimize the impact of change by maintaining familiar symbols. *Example:* When you move to a new job, bring along items you kept on your desk at your previous job.

⊠ Life is ongoing. You'll never have it under control, so stop trying.

⊠ Change is an inevitable part of life.

⊠ Saying *"I can't"* is a definite de-motivator. Instead use *"I can, if ... "*

⊠ The right attitude speeds the arrival of the desired results.

☒   By imagining how your life might be affected by a change, including the best and worst case scenarios, you can intellectually begin to make the change a potential reality.

☒   Changing your plans in the middle of a job is not a sign of defeat. It is a sign that you have found a better way based on knowledge you did not have when you started out.

☒   Schedule change if possible so you can anticipate its time of arrival and prepare in advance.

☒   Change should neither be overly feared nor overly embraced.

☒   If you invite change within yourself, rather than being affected by change, is easier to deal with.

☒   Don't turn away from a possibility of change until you are objectively sure it has nothing to offer.

☒   If you accept the security of inertia, you may lose the opportunity to change.

☒   Try something new every day to develop a tolerance for the new and different.

☒   Have a daily routine you can follow no matter what the circumstances or where you are. *Examples*: a morning jog, a half hour of reading before bed, a daily journal entry, a period of prayer or meditation.

☒   Obtain as much information as possible in advance so you can be fully prepared.

☒   Celebrate change.

☒   Seek out the support of those who have made a similar change. *Example*: People who have quit smoking, moved to a foreign country, started a new business. Learning what to expect makes change less frightening.

☒   It is usually easier to go with change than to fight against it.

☒   Resolve to pursue at least one new personal interest a month.

☒   Without first acknowledging that there is a problem, you can never fix it.

☒   When you tire of hobbies, activities or routines, retire them. Don't cling to worn out behaviors out of habit.

☒   When a change is frightening, focus on the concrete effects of the change rather than on your feelings about it.

☒   It is never too late to adjust to a change. If there is a change in your past that bothers you, take the time to look at how you could have handled it better and what you can do now to make it right.

☒   Set limits on what areas of your life a specific
change will or will not be allowed to affect.

☒   Treat change as an honored guest.

☒   In an ever changing world, what was satisfactory
yesterday, may be insufficient tomorrow.

☒   Tackle one major change at a time.

☒   If you must face a series of major changes, define
and deal with them independently.

☒   You can control the way change affects you and how
you respond to it, even if you cannot control the
change itself.

☒   If you cannot change your present situation, you can
always change your perspective.

☒   Know the consequences of failing to change.

☒   The ability to endure change helps you survive.

☒   Remember that change has brought you to where you
are now and will continue to help you grow if you
handle it deftly.

☒   Be positive.

☒   The ability to initiate change helps you thrive.

☒ You cannot change your actions without first changing how you think about those actions.

☒ Practice change. Change your hairstyle, change your breakfast cereal, change your jogging route.

☒ Write down all of the ways you can think of to minimize the negative effects of a change and put them to work.

☒ If you expect and plan for the discomfort of change, it is less daunting when it comes.

☒ Avoid being confined by self-made habits and rules.

☒ Practice adapting without changing your principles.

☒ Know how to achieve and leave. Don't cling to the past.

☒ Once you have committed to a change, avoid all temptations to turn back, including seemingly innocent ones.

☒ If you stop changing, you stop living.

☒ Life is a one way journey. No matter how badly you might want to go back, you cannot.

Motivate Others

☒   Provide opportunities to talk about an impending change to give people the chance to identify their feelings toward it.

☒   Identify the exact steps needed to cause the change. Often change is inhibited by misinformation.

☒   Change is more acceptable when it does not appear irrevocable.

☒   People change when they are good and ready to. You will never change someone who is not ready.

☒   Change is accepted better when those involved are treated as individuals with respect to how the change will affect them.

☒   Point out the difference between the real effects of the change and feelings about the change.

☒   Designate concrete areas that will not be affected by the change to create a psychological safety zone.

☒   Mark change with a celebration or ritual to signal its completion.

☒   Present a change in the most positive light, but don't hesitate to communicate potential negatives. Most people prefer to know both sides in advance so they are not shocked by a hidden negative later in the process.

☒   Once a change is made, encourage people to stick to it and avoid the temptation to revert to older, more comfortable ways.

☒   Change is easiest to face when you go through it with someone at your side.

☒   Point out the negative consequences of not changing.

☒   Allow sufficient time to adjust to change.

☒   Change brings four possible responses: acceptance, indifference, passive resistance, or active resistance.

☒   The acceptance of change is based not on the magnitude of the change but on the sensitivity of the presentation.

☒   Allow for mistakes and delays when a change is implemented. People quickly get frustrated if they feel you expect perfection from the start.

☒   Change is accepted better when those affected by it have some say in how it is implemented.

☒   Point out the habits and excuses that are preventing change from occurring.

☒   Outline some sample scenarios of the potential results of the change.

☒   Create an atmosphere that is open to regular change.

☒   Set a timetable for change so people can adjust their time related plans accordingly.

☒   Criticize people only about things they can do some-thing about. If they can't fix it, your criticism will be demoralizing and discourage their commitment to change.

☒   Change is accepted best when there is a logical reason behind it.

☒   Avoid implementing too many changes at once.

Chapter Ten

30 Ways to Motivate Conflict Resolution

30 Ways to Motivate Conflict Resolution

Lasting conflict resolution must be focused on producing a solution, not just getting rid of the problem.

Every day we are faced with conflicts, conflicts with family members, co-workers and even strangers on the street. Yet, how often do we truly solve the conflict, as opposed to just settling for getting rid of the problem? Sweeping the problem out of sight is certainly easier, but the results are temporary. The problem is buried just out of sight, ready to rear its head at the slightest prompting.

Conflict resolution requires effort and commitment. Whether you are trying to resolve a problem with someone else or between other parties, you will need all of your motivating skills to come to true conflict resolution.

Inspiration

- Every conflict is delightfully simple to resolve if the rewards are right.

- Remember that successful conflict resolution can unify two parties.

- The more options you collect, the greater chance that everyone will agree on one of them.

Application

- Before attempting to resolve a conflict, both parties should agree to consider all reasonable compromises.

- Focus on a few significant issues.

- Use positive body language by:

    a. sitting or standing straight and slightly forward
    b. keeping regular, but not intimidating, eye contact
    c. relaxing your arms and legs naturally
    d. acknowledging that you are listening by nodding your head from time to time

- Acknowledge that conflicts are bound to occur in groups because humans are intelligent, thinking beings.

- Focus on resolving, not eliminating, suppressing or avoiding the problem.

- Recognize that a conflict is a difference of views or opinions, not an insurmountable obstacle.

- Coordinate your body language and actions with your words to avoid sending conflicting signals.

- Try to resolve conflicts in a neutral setting, away from the root of the conflict and the participants' "home turf."

- Acknowledge that a resolution does not necessarily mean that everyone will be happy, but that they will be satisfied.

- Be willing to give in on some issues to motivate the other side to do the same.

- Honestly express your opinion.

- Don't confuse resolving the conflict with getting rid of the problem.

- Don't allow a conflict on one issue to destroy an entire relationship.

- Clarify perceptions and avoid stereotypes.

- Remove the preconception that conflict can be resolved only through one side winning and the other losing.

- Focus on solutions rather than problems or personal deficiencies.

- Be willing to start fresh without holding a grudge.

- Acknowledge intersecting points outside the conflict that may be common ground for resolution.

- Know the other party's motives at the outset.

- When mediating a conflict, lead others through the conflict resolution process without doing it for them.

- Give weight to the other party's emotions, which are potent factors in their decision making process.

- If you cannot negotiate a situation, set out to conquer it instead.

- Know what you want.

Chapter Eleven

56 Ways to Motivate Creativity

56 Ways to Motivate Creativity

Creativity is not a rare asset, we all possess some.

The gravest mistake we make in growing up is losing touch with our creative selves. Give a box of crayons and some paper to a five year old and he will unhesitatingly fill both sides with drawings and ask for more. Give the same crayons and paper to an adult and watch as the questions begin: What should I draw? What if no one knows what it is? What if I can't draw it well? Why am I doing this? How much time do I have to finish? Do I have to use both sides of the paper?

Many of us have lost touch with our innate creativity. It has not died or gone away, it is just dormant, buried under our adult sensibilities. Rediscovering the freedom to be creative, without the questions or doubts of adulthood, is one of the best gifts you can give yourself.

Inspiration

§   The very uniqueness of our being makes us creative. No two people are alike and neither are their ideas.

§   In the creation stage, nothing is wrong or right, you can go back and judge later.

§   Formal education is not a prerequisite to creativity, experience is.

§   To know and not use is the same as to not know.

§   Ideas only work if you do.

§   Create structure . . . adapt . . . let go . . . know when.

§   Unleash yourself.

§   Distrust of why you do things the way you do is the beginning of finding a better way.

§   There is always a better way.

§   If you are not making mistakes, you are not challenging your potential.

§   Creativity has two sources, the adaptation of known ideas and the creation of new ideas. The first is easily accepted and moderately successful. The second is generally rejected at first only to become the new standard in the future.

§   Without thought and intuition you cannot create.

§   Creativity is the construction of new roads on the ashes of conventional paths.

§   You never get a finished product on the first try.

§   Mistakes are not wasted effort, they are signposts on the road of creativity.

§   Sometimes a "hands-off" approach stimulates your subconscious creativity.

§   In general, creativity requires adaptation to make it acceptable to the masses.

§   Creativity means making do with what you have.

§   If you don't try it out, you'll never figure it out.

§   The more ideas you have, the more good ideas you will find.

§   Reinvent the familiar.

§   Creative doesn't mean complex.

§   Obstacles are the source of innovation.

§   Creative people experience more failures and make more mistakes, than those who never risk trying.

§   There is nothing new under the sun. When you realize this, you will know where creativity begins.

Application

§   Don't be confined by your plan, be open to whatever might happen along the way.

§   Rid your speech of cliches and take the time to really think about what you want to say in your own words.

§   Remove yourself from your daily routine or role.

§   In general, you are most creative when you don't feel you have to be.

§   Don't be intimidated by what others have created.

§   Never stop questioning the obvious.

§   Try a variation of freewriting. Set a time limit, say 20 minutes, and resolve to do your chosen activity unceasingly and without regard for quality until the time is up. Use this as a warm-up or to mine ideas from the resulting clutter.

§   When creating the new and different, unlearning is often more productive than learning.

§   Censor your sensory input and break the "garbage in-garbage out" cycle.

§   Give your mind the freedom to create.

§   Keep a journal to write down ideas as they arise. Use these ideas when you hit a dry spell.

§   Stop judging yourself and go with what you feel.

§   Constantly seek new experiences.

§   Throw the rules out the window.

§   Creativity requires refinement. Don't expect your brilliant ideas to be in their final form from the start.

§   When an idea nibbles at your mind, pull hard to hook it.

§   In the initial stages, produce quantity then go back and look for quality.

§   Creativity flourishes in a noncompetitive atmosphere.

§   Work from inside yourself.

§   Don't be afraid to look at a problem, walk away and come back later. Sometimes a little subconscious contemplation stirs the answer in your mind.

§   Surround yourself with creative people.

§   Don't get stuck on an idea that is going nowhere. Bring it to concrete reality or put it on the back burner and move on.

§   Be flexible.

§   Avoid relating new information to what you already know, instead try to see it objectively.

§   If you have to be creative on a deadline, provide yourself with a strong incentive, like the money you'll make from your idea, the fame you'll gain, the award you'll win.

§   Develop a broad range of interests.

§   Distance yourself from an idea through time, space, or thought.

§   Look at the creative people in your field. Are they smarter than you? Better than you? Probably not in every area. Find an area where you outshine them and imagine that if they can do it, so can you.

§   Use your routine chore time as thinking time. It's easy to think over a problem while you vacuum, ride a stationary bike, wait in traffic, ride the bus.

§   Give yourself enough uninterrupted time to concentrate on the creative process.

Chapter Twelve

44 Ways to Motivate Decision Making

44 Ways to Motivate Decision Making

Avoiding a decision is equal to deciding to do nothing.

The easy option in any situation is often to simply to avoid doing anything, to passively wait to see what happens. If you are willing to accept whatever fate brings you, this a great way of getting by. However, if you prefer to have some control over what happens in your life, you have to make decisions, big and small, hard and easy, good and bad.

When you choose to take on the responsibility of deciding, you give yourself several alternatives. Although they may not be the options you would ideally like to have, they are choices nonetheless. And when you have choices, you have control over the outcome. If you ever need the motivation to make a tough decision, consider the loss of control you face when choosing not to decide.

Inspiration

☒   Facts don't make decisions, people do.

☒   Once you cross the river, it's foolish to drag your boat across land.

☒   Consider other people's suggestions and opinions, but decide for yourself.

☒   If you have to spend twenty minutes deciding what to wear to work in the morning, you will take days or even weeks to make more serious decisions.

☒   Today's neglected decisions become tomorrow's crises.

☒   Delegating important decisions is just another way of avoiding them.

☒   Set free those options that you do not choose.

☒   Every decision has some painful side effects. If you try to make everyone happy, you may put off deciding indefinitely.

☒   There is no perfect answer.

☒   Analyze with your head, decide with your heart.

☒ Leave the realm of possibility behind and face the often less promising world of reality.

☒ Taking a wait-and-see attitude makes things worse as often as it makes them better.

☒ Deciding what not to do is as important as deciding what to do.

☒ Consider the consequences, but do not fear them.

☒ Decisions are easier to stick to when those around you know about them.

☒ Ignorance of your options leads to frustration.

☒ A decision without action is just a thought.

Application

☒   Accept the fact that nothing is certain and that no decision is perfect.

☒   If your decision is not going as planned, don't be afraid to admit your mistake and start over.

☒   Every decision must include a plan of action to carry out the decision.

☒   When you face a seemingly insoluble problem, go back to the beginning and retrace your steps. The most substantial answers are rarely something you haven't already thought of.

☒   A decision can always be modified or made up for if something goes wrong.

☒   Decide based on what you really need first and what you want second.

☒   You will never have enough information to decide flawlessly.

☒   Leave your emotions and personal biases at the door when making critical decisions.

☒   Have a fundamental understanding of an issue before you decide on it.

☒   The more successful you become, the more difficult
     decisions you will have to make. Readily accept
     every opportunity to practice along the way.

☒   Face your decision honestly.

☒   Don't decide based on what you wish the outcome to
     be but on the most likely outcome in reality.

☒   When you make a decision, set a target completion
     date to prevent procrastination.

☒   As much emphasis should be placed on implementing
     the decision as on making it.

☒   The more information you have, the more options
     you have to choose from.

☒   Face the facts head on.

☒   Once you decide, announce it. This will spur you
     to action.

☒   Sometimes it is best to make a decision based on
     your intuition. Intuition is created by the sum of
     many intangible and illogical concepts in your
     subconscious. It is the part of a decision you
     cannot deduce logically.

☒   Put your options on paper. Sometimes seeing things
     in writing makes them easier to organize and
     understand.

☒   Clarify generalities and identify biases.

☒   Execute big decisions as a series of smaller decisions and congratulate yourself on completing each step.

☒   Accept that decisions are made in reality and may require constraints, compromises or sacrifices.

☒   Strive to make the best choice for you right now, rather that waiting for an ultimate solution.

☒   Once you decide, set a specific start date within the next few days.

☒   Instead of asking yourself *"What should I do?"* (a question that translates to *"What do others think of my decision?"*), ask yourself *"What do I prefer?"* Indecision is often rooted in the difference between what you want to do and what others want you to do.

☒   Make a habit of the act of making decisions.

Chapter Thirteen

95 Ways
to
Motivate
Success

95 Ways to Motivate Success

Success is something you make happen, not something you let happen.

Success is the ultimate fulfillment of your desires, surely not something you need to be motivated to get. Or is it? Success is a vague term that often translates into "what I want, but don't yet have." In other words, whenever we achieve what we believed to be success, we find something bigger and better. And the meaning of success changes.

If you want to motivate yourself to be truly successful, you have to actively create your success, not wait for it to happen to you. And when you get what you want, you have to take the time to congratulate yourself and enjoy what you worked so hard for - before you set new goals and take off on another journey toward success.

Inspiration

⌘   Know where you are going, but never forget where you have been.

⌘   If you want to stand out in a crowd, you have to take a step out in front of it.

⌘   You'll never be here again.

⌘   Consistency breeds success.

⌘   The opportunities are right there, waiting for someone to make the most of them.

⌘   Success is the outcome of wise choices, adequate preparation and daring acts.

⌘   Success is within you, stop looking in the wrong places.

⌘   Knowing when to retreat is as important as knowing when to press ahead.

⌘   Failure is the predecessor of success.

⌘   Know your weakness not to lose, know your strength to triumph.

⌘   Great discipline breeds superior success.

⌘   A small success can release your fear of failure and motivate you toward greater success.

- ☿ Intelligent failure is better than foolish success.

- ☿ Success is built on two types of knowledge: acquired and self-awakened.

- ☿ Success does not require succeeding 100 percent of the time. Often, being successful 51 percent of the time is enough to win.

- ☿ There is no ultimate triumph, only a series of successes along the way.

- ☿ Don't blame failure when you have simply given up.

- ☿ Sometimes you have to lose a few battles to win the war.

- ☿ You learn more from your failures than from your successes.

- ☿ Time is gold and timing is diamond.

- ☿ The fool sits in the cave staring at the shadows on the wall. The wise man turns around and pursues the torch.

- ☿ Failure is not permanent - neither is success.

- ☿ Success is a daily practice of wise choices.

- ☿ Limit your expectations to the possible and you will meet them more often.

- Success is not what happens to you, it is what you do with what happens to you.

- See obstacles as the chance to learn to fly, not as roadblocks.

- Success is not a secure status, but a process toward a greater accomplishment.

- No problem endures the passing of time.

- A great idea requires a committed mind to carry it to maturity.

- If you fail to prepare, be prepared to fail.

- Keep your eyes fixed on the road to the top but don't assume you have arrived just because you   see the summit.

- You will become what you think you are worth.

- Failure is a sign that more effort is needed.

- Wealth is the by-product of success, not the goal.

- Success has to be nurtured more often than it is celebrated.

- One sacrifice today will bring two rewards tomorrow.

- Knowledge and application go hand in hand.

- Success comes one step at a time more often than it comes in one giant leap.

- You can be neither the first person ever to fail nor the last.

- You don't get to the top by waiting your turn.

Application

- Limit the number of detours you take from your chosen route to conserve your energy and reach your goal sooner.

- Fight boredom and apathy by trying something totally out of character.

- Stay focused on the present. Forget past failures and future roadblocks.

- Do what it takes to succeed in every moment.

- Stay focused on your goal.

- Follow the example of great people, past and present.

8   Measure success not in terms of other's praise or criticism, but in terms of your achievements in relation to your goals.

8   Refuse to lose.

8   Do what has to be done, especially when you don't feel like it.

8   You don't have to limit yourself to a single dream in life. The average person lives long enough to fulfill as many dreams as you like if you put your mind to it.

8   Success takes many forms and successful people recognize them all.

8   Success requires not just motivation but patience and tolerance.

8   Learn to recognize when the time is ripe for action. Everything has a peak and decline.

8   Delete "but" from your vocabulary.

8   Do what you know best and love most.

8   Don't forget your dream, even after it comes true.

8   If a past failure is preventing you from taking steps you need to reach your goals, look at the failure objectively as if you were giving advice to a friend.

- It is not impossible to break into a new field without credentials. The best way to get experience and make contacts is to volunteer.

- Learn something new every day.

- If you don't compete, you will never have the chance to win.

- Never stop challenging yourself. Create little challenges regularly. *Example:* Challenge yourself to run an extra half mile, to make an extra sales call, to add another facet to a presentation, to get up thirty minutes earlier, etc.

- Don't play to avoid losing, play to win.

- When you face a pivotal, high-anxiety moment, schedule some "anxiety time" in advance. *Example:* You have to make a guest appearance on a talk show that makes you very nervous. Arrive about ten minutes early and give yourself time to work off your nervousness by pacing the parking lot, singing to the radio or meditating in your car. When your anxiety time is over, leave your nervous feelings in the parking lot.

- To succeed in adversity you must expand yourself or contract the situation.

- Always be ready to erase your blackboard if a better idea comes along.

- Success requires a balance between knowledge that is acquired and knowledge that is self-awakened.

- Stop making excuses.

- Don't attach too much significance to any one goal or you will face an emotional let down when you reach it. More than one athlete has trained for years to win a major championship only to win and feel like *"This is it? This is what I sacrificed for?"* Fulfillment comes more from the process than from the result.

- Quit while you're ahead.

- Don't set out to conquer territory you can't defend.

- Long-term success is the result of success in each stage of the game.

- There is no map to success. Maps are made based on the landscape at a point in time. When the landscape changes, a new map must be created.   Do not believe that because it's on the map, it exists in reality. Keep your own map and update it frequently.

- Don't take no for an answer.

- Keep a success diary. When you are feeling down, review your "greatest hits."

- Practice being persistent - on yourself. Persistently shout down your own negative ideas and self talk until you run out of negativity.

- Remember that you are an adult and no one can really stop you from achieving your dreams unless you let them.

- Accept nothing less than excellence.

- Direction, purpose and discipline are essential to achieving your goals.

- There is nothing new under the sun. Doing something established well is a steadier road to success than creating something new.

- If you find yourself wandering from the path to success, go back to the fundamentals and replot your goals.

- You'll never have everything, so set priorities.

- If you must retreat from your goal, salvage as much as possible for another try in the future, when you are better prepared.

- Try and try again.

- Self-discipline gets you the last mile.

- The best route to success is hard work.

- Choose goals that are complementary or at least compatible. Having two major goals that conflict leaves you paralyzed by indecision. *Example:* You want to be independently wealthy by age thirty and you want to help inner city children reduce violence in their lives. Since social work is not a career that often leads to instant wealth, you obviously have to choose one or the other, at least for now.

- Don't be afraid to do what it takes to succeed, the dirty work and the glamourous work.

- Accept that the more successful you become, the less support and more animosity you will get from your colleagues.

- You succeed not for what you do, but for what people perceive you as doing.

- Assess setbacks honestly based on their overall impact on your efforts.

- Focus on creating your own perfect performance without regard to your competitors. If your performance is perfect, you will win naturally.

- Be willing to stand up and take responsibility for your mistakes.

- Don't be afraid of losing.

- Don't spend time reveling in your success when you should be plotting your next step.

Chapter Fourteen

39 Ways
to
Motivate
Leadership

39 Ways to Motivate Leadership

If you want someone to walk through the door,
you must open it first.

Mentoring, or motivating others to lead, is one of the most rewarding and powerful areas of leadership. The chance to act as a mentor is a challenging opportunity. Given the right candidate, you have the potential to develop a great leader for your company or organization and the opportunity to leave behind a legacy of your work.

To develop future leaders, you have to first let them see the possibility that lies within them and then open the door to their potential. Once you have given them a peek at the future, you need only steer them in the right direction, providing the occasional push on the uphill climb or applying the brakes if they accelerate too fast for the conditions.

Inspiration

➤ You can point the way, but in the end, each leader must walk alone.

➤ The seeds are only accessible when the mature fruit is broken open.

➤ The red rose is not as spectacular among a bouquet of roses as when it is placed in a vase of greens.

➤ Talented proteges do not outshine you, they light your way.

➤ Everyone has the potential for success. As a mentor, you have to find out where they are coming from, where they are going and when they need help along the way.

➤ Leaders must be mature in character to gain the respect of their subordinates.

➤ Leaders are developed most quickly under adverse conditions.

➤ Building leaders is a lifelong commitment.

➤ Leaders must want to lead. This is a fundamental quality you cannot teach.

➤ Leaders must be given the full authority they need to lead.

▲   Progressive challenges are essential in developing leaders.

▲   Leaders should be more intelligent than their subordinates, but not too much.

Application

▲   When selecting leaders, look for those who can take charge of a situation or group beyond being a role model.

▲   Give future leaders the work they need to develop skills and step up to greater responsibilities.

▲   Give clearly designated tasks that don't overlap with other leader's responsibilities.

▲   Remember that not everyone wants responsibility. Some people are leaders and others prefer to follow.

▲   Give potential leaders the chance to show off their stuff.

▲   Give future leaders the knowledge they need to not get sidetracked or squashed. Help them steer clear of politics, power struggles and back biting.

▲   Promote from within.

- ▲ People are more likely to take on leadership positions if they can "dress the part."

- ▲ Resist allowing your personal feelings to interfere with your professional decisions.

- ▲ Do not expect your leaders to produce more than you are willing to support them in producing.

- ▲ Occasionally risk delegating tasks that are above the potential leader's ability level to challenge him.

- ▲ Encourage future leaders to develop non-work related interests to broaden their personality.

- ▲ Allow potential leaders the chance to take charge in controlled situations so they can see their success at leading in a low risk situation.

- ▲ Have a long-term plan and be willing to invest in long term results.

- ▲ Give your protege the information needed to step-up, including insight into your leadership skills and abilities.

- ▲ Provide future leaders with character building opportunities.

- ▲ Let your protege see that you are like her in some way so she can envision herself in a position of authority like you.

▲   Provide additional incentives for those willing to assume leadership positions.

▲   Actively seek out leadership qualities in people. Many people have undeveloped potential for leadership.

▲   Don't expect your proteges to do your job for you.

▲   Allow potential leaders to witness leadership in action.

▲   Provide opportunities for both lateral and upward movement to broaden growth and sustain motivation.

▲   Give honest advice about strengths and weaknesses.

▲   Structure your mentoring as an ongoing, daily process.

▲   Clearly designate the apprentice's responsibilities for his growth.

▲   Treat people with average or potential abilities as though they are above average and watch as they begin behaving that way.

Chapter Fifteen

95 Ways
to
Motivate
Productivity

95 Ways to Motivate Productivity

*Motivation is the key to productivity. Given two people
of similar ability, the motivated person will always
outperform the unmotivated person.*

Procrastination is the graveyard of broken dreams. And motivation is the reincarnation of those dreams. Motivation lights a fire within you so you can overcome the urge to procrastinate and get started on the task at hand. When you learn to overcome the lure of the siren song of procrastination, your ability to accomplish your dreams is set free.

Inspiration

- 🕐 Seek problems because you need opportunities.

- 🕐 Being productive is one of the greatest intrinsic rewards.

- 🕐 Life goes on whether you fail or succeed at any single task.

- 🕐 You can do a lot with a little if that little is totally committed.

- 🕐 Working smart is always more productive than working hard.

- 🕐 Once you get going, the going gets easier.

- 🕐 Doing without thinking is as bad as thinking without doing.

- 🕐 A positive attitude is a poor substitute for actual preparation.

- 🕐 Organization invites work.

- 🕐 Remember to say "thank you" to yourself.

- 🕐 Aim for progress before perfection.

- 🕐 Effort alone is not enough, it must eventually produce measurable results.

🕐 Well begun is half done.

🕐 Activity is not the only necessity for productivity - thinking can be immensely productive.

🕐 Just because it doesn't have to be done now, doesn't mean you can't do it now.

Application

🕐 If you need to get something done and keep procrastinating, make an appointment with yourself and treat it as seriously as an appointment with your boss.

🕐 Don't get distracted by every "emergency" that comes along.

🕐 When you are very stressed over an impending deadline, remind yourself that nothing is so important that you should sacrifice your mental or physical health for it.

🕐 Look for opportunities to vary your work. *Example:* Produce your report in a new style, create a multi-media presentation instead of using overhead projectors, take a different route when making deliveries.

🕐   When there is something you absolutely have to do, but hate doing, get your frustration out in the open. Whine, gripe, complain and protest. Then use all of that energy you worked up to get the job done.

🕐   If you are avoiding a job because it is too big, divide it into manageable sections and complete them one at a time.

🕐   Stop waiting for the ideal time - it will never come.

🕐   Identify and challenge negative thoughts that are blocking your ability to get your job done.

🕐   Set priorities.

🕐   Write down the exact steps necessary to accomplish an undesirable task so you aren't tempted to get sidetracked.

🕐   Reserve your work area for work only - not coffee breaks, reading, or socializing.

🕐   Invest the most effort in those areas that produce the most results. Save non-productive tasks for your spare time.

🕐   Don't "manufacture" busy work to avoid what you should really be doing.

🕐   To get started on a major project, begin with a small or easy-to-complete task to establish your mental commitment to the job.

⊕   Beat procrastination by setting up guilt-free time to "goof off" as a reward for successfully finishing a task you usually avoid.

⊕   Learn to say *no* to tasks you don't have time for or interest in.

⊕   Do not wait for some kind of intangible inspiration to start your task. Get started on the easiest part and the inspiration may come along the way.

⊕   Do the task you are in the proper frame of mind to do - social, analytical, creative, routine, etc.

⊕   Substitute rational thoughts for time wasting excuses. *Example:* Instead of thinking *"This project has to be perfect"* try *"I would like really like this project to turn out perfectly, so I should get started while I have plenty of time to devote to it."*

⊕   Act on an idea when it occurs. The farther you get from the initial emotional spark, the less likely you are to follow through. To set an idea in motion:
          a. phone someone about it
          b. write a memo
          c. make an action plan
          d. make an outline
          e. talk to someone about it
          f. list key ideas
          g. budget it
          h. enlist assistance
          i. delegate it

⏲   Do one thing at a time.

⏲   If you're having trouble getting started, make an irrevocable commitment. *Example*: You keep meaning to clean out your garage and have a tag sale, but never seem to get around to it. Get yourself motivated by calling up your local newspaper and placing an ad for your tag sale. Now you have both a deadline and motivation to get started.

⏲   Make a daily "to do" list and set priorities in order of importance.

⏲   Use your answering machine to screen calls. You don't have to worry about missing emergency calls and you won't be tempted to waste time on unimportant calls.

⏲   Close your office door.

⏲   When it's done, forget it and move on.

⏲   Build in break time for stress relief.

⏲   Avoid announcing your plans in advance, it brings out the opposition in droves.

⏲   Do it right the first time, even if it takes longer.

⏲   "What if.." is all right in the planning stage, but once a plan is established, drop the "ifs" and focus on what must be done.

- When you are under emotional stress, focus on task-oriented jobs that can be completed without emotional or creative input.

- Always carry something with you to do while you wait for meetings to start, for appointments, etc.

- Be your own cheerleader. When you finish a tough task, get excited, jump up and down, give yourself a high five, sing a song. You may feel silly but you will definitely not feel tired, frustrated, anxious or stressed.

- Having an underlying reason to accomplish what you want is the best motivator. Cleaning the house because your boss is coming to dinner produces better results than cleaning because you have a vague notion that you have to. If your boss isn't really coming for dinner, pretend that he is!

- Know the limits of your job. Don't waste time duplicating other people's work.

- Eliminate unnecessary procedures and bureaucracy. If you cannot identify a direct benefit of a system, procedure or requirement, eliminate it.

- Give yourself a comfortable amount of time to finish a task and promise yourself a break if you finish early. *Example*: If you can easily finish your report in an hour, by fully concentrating you can finish in forty minutes and take a twenty minute break.

🕐   Hang up a motivational saying or other motivating visual reminder in your car, workplace, or office.

🕐   Don't spend inordinate amounts of time on low priority tasks.

🕐   Simplify your work area by starting a clutter box for things you don't have a place for - all those things you might need for something, but have no idea for what.

🕐   Contract out portions of your work to independent professionals.

🕐   Separate thinking time from working time.

🕐   When faced with a monotonous task, make a game of it. See how much you can finish in ten minutes. Try to beat that amount in the next ten minutes and so on.

🕐   If you find yourself doing meaningless time wasters to avoid a task, try doing nothing. You will soon find yourself anxious to do anything, including the task you found so repelling.

🕐   Don't leave loose ends. You can spend more time avoiding tying them up than you would have to finish them up in the first place.

🕐   Take a step-by-step approach and emphasize successful completion of short-term goals.

- ⏲ When you can't motivate yourself to get a job done, list the benefits of doing it versus the reasons for not doing it. See which side is more compelling.

- ⏲ Don't spend time on projects that you are stuck on, instead come back to them later.

- ⏲ Group similar tasks together. *Example*: run all errands together, return all phone calls at the same time, answer mail as you open it.

- ⏲ The longer you wait, the more ominous and unpleasant a task seems. It's much less stressful to "bite the bullet" and get it done now.

- ⏲ Don't allow people to waste your time with unsolicited sales calls, unwanted social visits, etc.

- ⏲ Delegate routine and menial tasks.

- ⏲ Delegate work that can be done by others, starting with the jobs you dislike most.

- ⏲ Go for a walk or jog when your energy is waning. It will enliven your body and your mind.

- ⏲ If a task is overwhelming in size, even when broken down into smaller goals, commit to spend a specific period on it - say an hour per day or two days each week.

- ⏲ Avoid delegating work you enjoy.

🕐   If you aren't blessed with self-discipline, pretend you are.

🕐   Identify the real cause behind your procrastination and attack it head-on. The job will get done in the process.

🕐   You can remove four common excuses for procrastination if you:
>   Have the tools you need to get the job done,
>   know where they are,
>   have enough of them,
>   and keep them in working order.

🕐   When possible, choose projects that relate to your personal interests or talents.

🕐   Keep unnecessary distractions out of your work area.

🕐   When you are having a hard time getting around to a task of moderate importance, schedule a specific time to do it instead of leaving it to chance.

🕐   Create an environment in which you can display the efforts of your work. Enter your ad design in a contest, apply for a research grant, submit your article to a magazine.

🕐   Save routine tasks for times when you are not up for more challenging work.

🕐   When you can't find enough hours in the day to finish

your work, keep a work diary. Write down what you
did and the amount of time it took. After two weeks,
look for patterns of wasted time, bad habits, disorga-
nization, procrastination, etc.

Establish a system for handling incoming paper to
limit the number of times you handle it. (Once is
best, more than twice is a major time waster.)

Write down a task and forget about it until the time
comes to do it.

If you have trouble getting off the phone, get an
hourglass type timer and use it to limit unimportant
calls.

1001

Right now, close your eyes and finish this sentence:

"I've always wanted to _____."

Now, go get started.

About the Author

In just ten short years, author Sang H. Kim has risen to international acclaim in his field, doing what he loves. As a young boy, he dreamed of coming to America from his native Korea. Now, in less than a decade in his new home, he has become one of the premiere international stars in the martial arts world. His rise as a coach, teacher, lecturer, author and mentor has been nothing short of inspiring.

Rising above the struggles of adapting to a new culture, he has achieved such diverse accomplishments as starting two successful business, establishing a college course, training an Olympic champion, presenting seminars across the country and the world, authoring eight books, producing dozens of video tapes and films, starting an innercity youth self-esteem building program, and yet he still finds time to give a motivational speech at his town's middle school at the start of every school year.

The key to his success, he believes, lies in finding the motivation to make the most of every day, every hour. In *1,001 Ways to Motivate Yourself and Others*, he shares his favorite motivational tips and inspirational sayings with you.